UPROARIOUS
Riddles
FOR
MINECRAFTERS

MOBS, GHASTS, BIOMES, AND MORE!

BRIAN BOONE

Illustrations by Amanda Brack

Sky Pony Press
New York

Copyright © 2018 by Hollan Publishing, Inc.

Minecraft® is a registered trademark of Notch Development AB.

The Minecraft game is copyright © Mojang AB.

Sky Pony Press books may be purchased in bulk at special discounts for sales promotion, corporate gifts, fund-raising, or educational purposes. Special editions can also be created to specifications. For details, contact the Special Sales Department, Sky Pony Press, 307 West 36th Street, 11th Floor, New York, NY 10018 or info@skyhorsepublishing.com.

Sky Pony® is a registered trademark of Skyhorse Publishing, Inc.®, a Delaware corporation.

Visit our website at www.skyponypress.com.

10 9 8 7 6 5 4 3 2 1

Library of Congress Cataloging-in-Publication Data is available on file.

Cover illustration by Amanda Brack
Cover design by Brian Peterson

Paperback ISBN: 978-1-5107-2717-5
Ebook ISBN: 978-1-5107-2722-9

Printed in Canada

UPROARIOUS
Riddles
FOR
MINECRAFTERS

MOBS, GHASTS, BIOMES, AND MORE!

Also by Brian Boone:

Hysterical Jokes for Minecrafters: Blocks, Boxes, Blasts, and Blow-Outs, Book 3

Side-Splitting Jokes for Minecrafters: Ghastly Golems and Ghoulish Ghasts, Book 4

Gut-Busting Puns for Minecrafters: Endermen, Explosions, Withers, and More!, Book 6

The Know-It-All Trivia Book for Minecrafters: Over 800 Amazing Facts and Insider Secrets

The Unofficial Harry Potter Joke Book: Great Guffaws for Gryffindor

CONTENTS

INTRODUCTION

See if you can solve this riddle:

What's the most popular game in the world?

What's like playing with blocks, but is also like playing in a sandbox?

What's a lovely place to build a home . . . even though it's full of monsters?

Give up? It's *Minecraft,* of course. The video game and its immersive world created by the mighty Notch has delighted millions around the world over the past decade. Just as delightful: jokes, wordplay, and especially riddles all about *Minecraft.* Presenting *Uproarious Riddles for Minecrafters: Mobs, Ghasts, Biomes, and More.* It's the latest in our *Jokes for Minecrafters* series, and you'll find hundreds upon hundreds of jokes about everything that makes *Minecraft* so special, from Steve and Alex to blocks and ores to Skeletons, Zombies, Creepers, and everything else in between.

You're sure to find all kinds of stuff in *Uproarious Riddles for Minecrafters* to keep yourself and all your friends both laughing and guessing. So what are you waiting for? *Dig* in!

CHAPTER 1

WHAT AM I?

I like to swim, I like to fly
I like to walk, I love to try . . .
But you only see me when I die.
What am I?
Fish.

■

I'm red, blue, anything you want me to
I reach the sky, quite so high.
What am I?
Fireworks.

■

As brittle as the sand, but hard as rock
I'll take you to a new place, and then back.
What am I?
Obsidian.

You can eat me, and I'm orange, but in *Minecraft,* there are no oranges.
What am I?
A carrot.

You built me but I will destroy you.
What am I?
TNT.

I'm like a daisy
And I'm always wavy
I'm a special kind of flower
That has a fair amount of power.
What am I?
Poppy.

Send me away
But I will come back
Use me the right away
I'll provide a nice snack.
What am I?
Fishing rod.

Amidst the chaos, there I stand
Never warm, yes I am cold
Come to me, full of life
And thus begins your time of strife.
What am I?
The End.

I can be black or white
I'm small, and I don't bite
I'm soft, I walk . . . if I'm all right.
What am I?
Sheep.

Grumble, grumble
I always mumble.
What am I?
A ghast.

Hot like fire, float like a breeze?
I come from a mob
A fiery blob.
What am I?
A ghast fireball.

I'm sad but not blue
I'm friendly but not to you
Sorry for what I'm about to do—
BANG!
What am I?
A creeper.

I like to hide, I like to swim
I'll get close to you, if that's my whim!
What am I?
Silverfish.

I can hold a ton of treasures, more than you ever would think
    possible. Don't leave me unattended—I'll go fast!
What am I?
A Chest.

■

I am as numerous as the stars,
I can be used to tell time
Or create a sculpture.
What am I?
Sand.

■

I don't like Creepers
So I'll get them from standing away many meters.
What am I?
Bows and arrows.

■

I shine but not so bright
My brethren shines brighter.
What am I?
A redstone torch.

I beep, I bop, I thud, I thwop.
What am I?
A Note Block.

■

I am devastatingly destructive, and yet I am unarmed. What am I?
A Creeper.

■

I fly through the sky and maybe right through you. But I am not a ghost. What am I?
A Ghast.

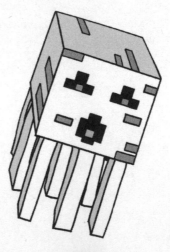

I live though I am dead. What am I?
A Zombie.

Don't get all hot and bothered trying to figure out what I am!
A Blaze.

When you're with me, you stop on green and go on red.
    What am I?
A Watermelon!

I'm a *Minecraft* thing that's full of ticks . . . but I'm not a
    Dog or a Wolf. What am I?
A Clock.

I don't have any "armies" but I can destroy you just the
    same. What am I?
A Creeper.

I am but one, but I wear many hats. What am I?
A Wither.

■

I have many rings but no fingers. What am I?
A Tree.

■

Open your eyes and you will not see me.
Close your eyes and you will. What am I?
Darkness.

■

I rattle, but a baby wouldn't like me. What am I?
A Skeleton.

■

I'll make you hungry while grossing you out at the same
time. What am I?
A Husk.

I like to attack, but if I'm not attacking, you're attacking me, and then I'm running away from the attack. What am I?
An Evoker.

■

I am evoked, but I am not an Evoker. What am I?
A Vex.

■

I can stand in the sun all day, but my skin doesn't burn. What am I?
A Husk.

■

I can give you the power to walk through walls. What am I?
A door.

■

I'm orange on top and white on the bottom. What am I?
A Snow Golem.

I'll offer you a tip, but you should always turn it down—and
quickly. What am I?

A Stray (with a slowness-inflicting arrow).

■

I make a noise once . . . but you'll hear me over and over
again. What am I?

A stray (stray . . . stray . . . stray . . .).

■

I am like a Torch, but I am not a Torch Block. What am I?

A Jack-O-Lantern.

I have six sides, but I am but one thing. What am I?
A Block!

■

I am a Hostile, except when I'm a building Block. What am I?
Slime.

■

I am the only Ore that can't be mined with a tool made out of myself. What am I?
Gold ore.

■

If you can't see in the sea, I can help you see in the sea, if you can see enough in the sea to see me. What am I?
A Sea Lantern.

■

I am a Block, but you can't hold me, place me, or mine me, or see me. What am I?
An air block.

I have lots of eyes but cannot see. What am I?
A potato.

■

I am a rock, but am softer than dirt. What am I?
Netherrack.

■

I'm a crop and provide energy, and you may think I could help you walk, but I can't. What am I?
Sugar cane.

■

I fly high in the nether, and the Ender dragon is my mortal enemy. What am I?
Wither.

■

When you see a potion, trouble is brewing. What am I?
A witch.

■

I come in a Hostile Mob of three . . . but I am not a trio of witches. What am I?
Wither.

I'm wet, but I'm not a River or an Ocean. I am land but I am not the Desert or the Forest. What am I?
Swampland.

■

If you want to come to this biome, you'll just have to go with the flow. What am I?
River.

■

Wooden you like to know which biome I am?
Forest.

■

My name means ordinary but I'm anything but. What am I?
Plains.

■

I am high, but not mountain high. What am I?
Extreme Hills.

If you want to visit me, dry, dry again. What am I?
Desert.

■

A newfound wave of excitement will wash over you when
visiting me. What am I?
Ocean.

■

I'm up above you and all around, but I'm also where the
story goes no further. What am I?
The End.

■

I am a block but I am not
You can see me, but you cannot
I exist, that much is true
Air Block.

■

I am blue, with a heart of gold
I am new, still I look old
Deep in the water, so you're told
Ocean Monument.

WHAT AM I?

Am I really that disgusting?
I only want a part of you
I have no use for all of you
 . . . or I'll just find somebody new
Zombie.

■

A visit here is like a day at the, well, you know. What am I?
Beach.

■

Don't bungle this or you'll die on the vine.
Jungle.

CHAPTER 2

A MOB OF HOSTILE MOB JOKES

How do Guardians stay healthy?
Plenty of Vitamin Sea.

■

Why do Withers look so tough?
Because they wear Wither jackets.

■

What's a Shulk's favorite superhero?
The Incredible Shulk!

■

Why did the Skeleton shoot his arrows?
Because he's heartless.

A fiery Hostile attacked a Cow in the plains every day for a few weeks.
It was an amazingly crazy Blaze graze phase!

Skeletons have a hard time making friends.
They're such lonely boneys.

Slime think everybody loves them. Whenever they come up it's always "ooze" and "aggggghhhhhs!"

What makes the Guardian special among Hostiles?
It's very so-fish-ticated.

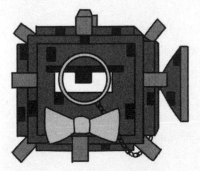

What time do you see Zombies in *Minecraft*?
At ate o'clock.

■

Why did the Zombie eat the Skeleton?
He wanted his bone and marrow.

■

How can you always beat a Zombie?
If you're the kind of person who has to get the last sword in.

■

Why wasn't the Vex much of an opponent?
It was flew season.

■

What floats and hisses?
A Ghast that learned how to speak Creeper.

■

Why don't Skeletons like the summer?
They're afraid of sunburns.

Why did the Ghast invade a tower?
It was in high spirits.

∎

What's the most dangerous job in *Minecraft*?
Being an Evoker's dentist.

∎

Can you name 30 creatures from *Minecraft*?
29 Creepers and a Ghast.

∎

What's the heaviest mob in *Minecraft*?
Skele-tons.

∎

What day are Zombies most likely to attack?
Chewsday.

∎

What do Shulkers like on their pizza?
Purpuroni.

What do you call the first player who discovered a Blaze?
Toast!

■

Why do the Witches wear black hats?
To keep their heads warm.

■

Where do Zombie Pigmen buy their weapons?
Hamazon!

■

What kind of tests do Vexes take?
Vexaminations.

■

How do Vexes learn to fly?
They just wing it.

■

What's the difference between a fly and a Vex?
A Vex can fly, but a fly can't Vex.

Why couldn't the Zombie Pigman get out of lava?
Because he was a slow-pork.

How do Skeletons remain so calm when they're attacking?
Because nothing gets under their skin!

Will Shulkers always blend into their purpur shells to hide?
Yep, you can be Shulk they will!

■

What do a Blaze and a light source have in common?
One will scorch and the other is a Torch.

■

How did the Spider find a Spider Jockey?
It asked its hairy godmother.

■

How do you stop a Zombie Pigman?
Put him in hamcuffs.

■

How do Guardians fight off invaders?
Very e-fish-iently.

■

How does a Shulker talk to other Shulkers?
With a shell phone.

What happened when the Magma Cube wandered into an icy biome?
There was a lava-lanche!

■

Why did the Magma Cube attack?
It's just his way of saying, "I lava you."

■

Where do Magma Cubes go to the bathroom?
The lava-tory.

■

What do Magma Cubes eat?
Anything with lots of f-lava.

■

Why are Creepers so angry?
You would be too if you had green skin, no arms, and could explode at a moment's notice.

What do you get when you cross a Shulker with a Guardian?
A Hostile that is very shell-fish.

How do Shulkers know when the player is approaching?
They use a shelloscope.

Where's the best place to learn about Witches?
Witchapedia.

Where's the best place to learn about how Hostile cubes work?
In a Magmazine.

What did the overworked Evoker do?
It decided to lay low for a while.

What did the Skeleton say when he ran out of arrows?
"Shoot."

When something in *Minecraft* seems fishy . . . it's probably a
Guardian.

Did you hear about Steve getting the Evoker with a sword?
It was his trusty Evoker Poker.

Did you hear about the Hostile who snuck onto Steve's boat?
It was a Ghast by the mast.

How do Guardians keep their breath fresh?
With monu-mints.

Why are Withers so good at baseball?
They always turn out a triple play.

Why are Ghasts white?
Because they got so afraid when they saw another Ghast!

What is a Vex's dream car?
A Vexus.

What do a fang-armed Hostile and Chickens have in common?
One's an Evoker, and one's a yolker.

What's an Evoker's favorite holiday?
Fangs-giving.

What kind of parties do Evokers like best?
Teeth parties.

How do Evokers stay healthy?
Bite-amins.

Where do you find a Skeleton?
Just follow the arrows.

When are you most likely to run into Skeletons?
During the graveyard shift.

■

What do you call it when a Skeleton drops something valuable?
A bone-us!

■

Why should you stay away from a Vex?
Because smoking is bad for you!

■

Where do Desert Zombies shop for their clothes?
In the Husk-y section.

■

What are rotten but not forgotten?
Husks.

■

Why did the Desert Zombies stalk Steve?
Husk because!

Why did the Husk go to the desert?
Because it heard it was the hot place to be!

What will a Vex attack?
What have you got?

How do you get a Vindicator to attack?
Just axe!

What do you call a stray?
Chilled to the bone!

When's the one time you'll always run into an Evoker?
Tooth-hurty.

What did the Evoker say after it bit Steve?
"Fangs!"

What do you call a Desert Zombie's odor?
A Husk musk.

Why do Husks sound so raspy?
They eat a lot of rasp-berries.

What's the difference between *Minecraft* and an Evoker?
One has bytes and the other has bites.

What did Steve say to the Vindicator when he needed emeralds?
"Can't we just drop this?"

Where do Vexes live?
Vexico.

What goes *clang bang*?
A Creeper holding a bell.

What do you get when you cross an Evoker and a Skeleton?
A Hostile that bites your knees.

Why didn't the Evoker eat a big meal?
He just wanted a few bites.

What do you call a Guardian with no eye?
A Guardan.

■

What's the difference between a Guardian and an Ocelot?
One drops fish . . . and the other never would!

■

What do you call it when a Guardian squeaks so loud that it
   summons another Guardian?
A squeakuel.

■

How can you have stairs underwater?
When it's a Guardian and they're stares.

■

What's the difference between an especially fiery hostile and
   a Guardian?
One is a Blazer, and the other has a laser.

What should you never make with a Guardian?
Eye contact!

■

What kind of structures could Guardians build with?
Laser beams!

■

Where do Shulkers power up?
At the Shell Station.

■

What's a Shulker's favorite old album?
Purpur Rain.

■

What's a Shulker's favorite game?
Hide-and-Hide.

■

What's a Shulker's favorite kitchen gadget?
A blender.

Why is the Guardian such an effective Hostile?
Because of its laser-like focus!

Why was the Skeleton after the miner?
He had a bone to pick.

Where do Evokers and Vindicators live?
In a nice Illage.

What did Steve say when he grabbed some dropped Emeralds?
"Finally, I've been Vindicator-ated!"

Why didn't the Guardian attack?
Out of sight, out of mind.

What does a Ghast do on the Internet?
It twects.

What do you get if you cross a monkey and a Creeper?
A baboom!

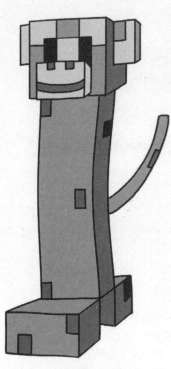

What's more annoying than a Skeleton shooting bows and
  arrows at you?
Ten Skeletons shooting bows and arrows at you.

Why did the Creeper never get called on in school?
Because it never raised its hand.

Why can't you trust a Zombie Pigman?
They always squeal.

Why do Witches like football?
For all the huts.

Who's a Zombie Pigman's favorite artist?
Pig-casso

What's white, floaty, and wears sunglasses?
A Ghast on vacation.

Where do Blazes eat?
At Sizzler.

CHAPTER 3

FOOD, FARMS, AND FARMERS

What do Creepers eat for breakfast?
Sssssscrambled eggs.

■

How do Creepers get in their vegetables each day?
With a big ssssssalad.

■

What drink should be avoided at all costs in *Minecraft*?
"Tea and tea."

■

Why did the Farmer plant blocks of Hay?
He wanted straw berries.

What's the most dangerous Easter candy in *Minecraft*?
Marshmallow Creeps.

■

The creator of *Minecraft* eats this for lunch.
Notch-os.

■

What do Miners eat at the movies?
Gemmy Bears.

■

What did Steve say after he ate a sheep?
"I can't believe I ate the wool thing!"

■

How do Minecrafters start their day?
With a cup of Builders' tea.

■

What do Minecrafters eat at 4 p.m.?
Tea and stones.

What do Minecrafters put in their tea?
Sugar cubes.

What kind of cookies does Steve eat?
Ore-e-os.

How are plants in *Minecraft* like math?
The square roots.

■

What kind of food might you find atop a wall?
A wall-nut.

■

What do they serve in the Ice Plains Biome?
Chili!

■

What do Creepers eat for breakfast?
Rice Creepies.

■

What do you call a smiling Pumpkin?
A pumpgrin!

■

How do Ghasts make sandwiches?
With fresh dread.

What kind of milk do you get from a pampered cow?
Spoiled milk.

■

What do you get from a Cow in the Tundra Biome?
Ice cream.

■

How can you tell if a Minecrafter has been eating your
  sandwich?
There are "8 bits" taken out of it.

■

What do Spiders in abandoned mineshafts eat?
Corn on the cobwebs.

■

What are all meals in *Minecraft*?
Square meals.

■

What do you feed trees in *Minecraft?*
Knuckle sandwiches.

Where does a Minecrafter eat cookies?
Mrs. Fields.

Where does a Minecrafter buy chocolate?
Rocky Mountain Chocolate Company.

Where does Steve eat burgers?
Steve-in-the-Box.

Where does Steve get burgers and shakes?
Shake Shack.

What cool rock n' roll restaurant do Minecrafters like?
The Hard Rock Café.

What's red and cold?
An apple in a cold biome.

What ice cream do Minecrafters eat?
Rocky Road.

What do *Minecraft* ore eat?
Pom-a-granites.

What's a Minecrafter's favorite cereal?
Cocoa Pebbles.

What's a Minecrafter's favorite candy?
Rock candy.

How does Steve like his soda?
On the rocks!

What fruit prevents Steve from catching a cold?
Ore-anges.

What kind of fish do Minecrafters like best?
Walleye.

How did Notch fix a glitch in the farming elements of the game?
With a cabbage patch.

What's a Minecrafter's favorite baked dessert?
Cobbler.

What kind of salad is served in the colder biomes?
Ice-berg lettuce.

How do Minecrafters take their pizza?
Plain.

What do you feed an Enderman?
Evaporated milk.

What's a Minecrafter's favorite kind of cheese?
Swiss, because it's full of holes.

What's a Minecrafter's *other* favorite kind of cheese?
Cottage cheese.

Why didn't the Minecrafter have to pay for dinner?
It was on the house!

What do you feed a Sword?
Slice cream.

What will spawn if you plant seeds at night?
Moonbeams.

Where do crops hang out before they sprout?
The Wheating room.

What do Farmers eat for breakfast?
Wheaties.

What *Minecraft* room can you not enter?
A mushroom.

What did the Fishing pole say to the Fish?
"Catch you later!"

What is green and jumps?
A Watermelon with hiccups!

What's brown and has wheels?
Wheat. (We were kidding about the wheels.)

What do Minecrafters order at a Mexican restaurant?
An ore-ito.

Did you hear about the carrots that were about to fall off
Steve's workbench?
They were some edgy veggies.

What did Steve take to eat during a mining day?
A boxed lunch.

What do Minecrafters collect?
Lunchboxes.

What side dish do Minecrafters love?
Coal slaw.

Where do Minecrafters go to have buffet?
Golden Corral.

Why didn't the Minecrafter like dropped meat?
It was a little too raw for him.

What do Minecrafters eat for lunch?
Minekraft Macaroni and Cheese.

What did the glowstone eat for lunch?
Just a light meal.

How do Minecrafters keep their breath fresh?
With develop-mints.

Where do Rabbits go to eat?
IHOP.

How do you make lemons in *Minecraft*?
Rearrange the "Melons."

Why couldn't the Minecrafter make any more sugar cane?
She was out of stalk.

Why couldn't the Minecrafter make any more sugar cane?

What crop do you never have a little of?
Cocoa—because you wind up with a choco-lot of it.

What potato chips do Minecrafters eat?
Roofles.

Why did the Minecrafter plant potatoes and carrots?
He wanted to get back to his roots.

What did Alex say when Steve brought her fresh sugar cane?
"That's sweet!"

What drink will you find underground in *Minecraft*?
Coal-a.

How long does it take crops to grow in Farmland?
About a wheat.

How long does it take crops to grow in Farmland?
About a wheat.

Why did the player hide his chest in Farmland?
He was playing Crops and Robbers.

What crop is the most fun to grow?
Wheeeeeeeat!

What happened when cocoa got planted near an Ender Dragon?
Cocoa Puffs!

What's brown, round, and found underground?
Potatoes.

Which mushrooms should you use in *Minecraft*?
We don't know, it's soup to you!

What do Minecrafters eat for breakfast?
Dragon eggs and Beacon.

What happened when Steve ate too many pickles?
He turned into Herobrine.

What kind of chocolates do Minecrafters prefer?
Bomb-bombs.

What's another way to get gold in *Minecraft*?
Find 24 carrots!

Why was the farm upset?
It was just irrigated.

Where would you find corn in *Minecraft*?
In a Cobweb block.

This room can only be brown or red. What kind of room is it?
A mushroom.

In what video game can you grow pickles?
Brinecraft.

What do Minecrafters order at barbecue restaurants?
A slab of anything.

CHAPTER 4

WHAT'S THE DIFFERENCE?

What's the difference between a fruit crop and a Note Block?
One is Melon-y, and the other plays a melody.

What's the difference between Antarctica and the Ice Plains?
One is a no man's land, and the other is a snowman's land.

What's the difference between a bully and Obsidian?
One is the toughest guy on the block and the other is the
toughest Block on a guy.

What's the difference between school and *Minecraft*?
One is boring, and the other is ore-ing.

What's the difference between an Enderman and a house?
One hates stares and the other has stairs.

What's the difference between a Cow and a Chicken?
One drops leathers and the other drops feathers.

What's the difference between a Tree and an Evoker?
The bite is worse than the bark!

What's the difference between a Horse and a Skeleton?
One was a pony, and the other is quite bony.

What's the difference between a tamed Ocelot and a Shulker?
One likes to purr and the other likes purpurs.

What's the difference between a Cow and a Creeper?
One moos and one moosssssss.

What's the difference between a lighted block and a Vex?
One is a beacon and the other is beakin'.

What do Australia and the Nether have in common?
They're both Down Under!

Which weighs more, a ton of Redstone or a ton of Glowstone?
They *both* weigh a ton.

How is an Enderman like an oyster?
It's hard to get them to give up their Pearls.

What do a Dog's tail and a minecart have in common?
One's a waggin' and the other's a wagon.

What do Parrots and parents have in common?
They don't like you playing too much *Minecraft*!

What's the difference between a Witch's potion, and some
 Obsidian?

One is a bracken brew and the other is black and blue.

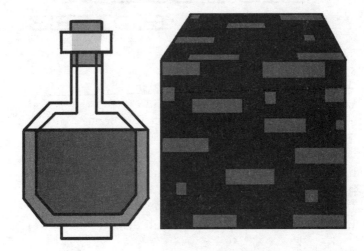

CHAPTER 5

BIOMES AND OTHER HOMES

What state would Minecrafters like to visit?
Minersota.

What Colorado city could a Minecrafter live?
Boulder.

What California area would appeal to Steve?
Pebble Beach.

What Georgia city sounds like a biome?
Savannah.

What Arizona city sounds like a biome?
Mesa.

■

What mountain range sounds the most *Minecraft*-y?
The Rocky Mountains.

■

This place where four states meet sounds like a *Minecraft*
feature.
Four Corners.

■

This Nordic country sounds like a biome.
Iceland.

■

This large island also sounds like it could be a biome.
Greenland.

■

Why did the Minecrafter enjoy *The Wizard of Oz*?
Because of the Emerald City.

Which Pennsylvania city sounds like it's full of mines?
Pittsburgh.

■

This is the capital of Arkansas, and could also be a *Minecraft* thing.
Little Rock.

■

Minecrafters would love this Illinois city.
Rockford.

■

This west coast state is home to lots of Minecrafters.
Ore-gon.

■

This city in Michigan isn't *entirely* made of ore.
Flint.

■

Is this Southwestern state a *Minecraft* paradise?
Ore-izona.

This city in Texas has definitely got to be a biome.
Grand Prairie.

■

This city in Kansas sounds like it came straight out of
Minecraft.
Overland Park.

■

If the major Texas city of San Antonio was located in
Minecraft, it would be called . . .
Sand-and-Stony-O.

■

Is this an island, or an 8-bit item?
Cube-a.

■

This Southwestern state might be full of trees.
Oak-lahoma.

■

This California town might also have a lot of Wood ready to go.
Oak-land.

This famous city in Louisiana might have lots of rocks and gems.
New Ore-leans.

This famous city in Louisiana might have lots of rocks and gems.
New Ore-leans.

Minecrafters looking for a vacation might visit this place in Mexico.
Rockapulco.

What did the Canadian Minecrafter call the biome they'd never seen?
Newfoundland.

What's the best thing to do in the Ice Biome?
Chill.

Why is the Ocean Biome blue?
Because it's under the weather.

How did the Skeleton get to a grassy biome?
He took an arrow-plane.

Where do Ghasts get their strength?
At the Ghast station.

Where do Witches Spawn?
In Wichita.

Where do Blazes spawn?
In Phoenix.

Which biome has the worst popsicles?
The Ice Plains.

■

Why does Steve look out the window in the morning?
Because he couldn't see through the wall.

■

What happened to the Minecrafter's computer when he went
to the Ice Biome?
It froze.

■

Why didn't Steve want to explore the ocean?
There was something fishy about it.

■

Which is the best biome to take a nap?
The For-rest.

■

How do you play *Minecraft* in the sky?
With an air-craft.

How do you play *Minecraft* in the ocean?
With a water-craft.

■

It has a mouth but can't eat. What is it?
A river!

■

What has a bed but doesn't sleep?
A river.

■

What's the most valuable part of a river?
The banks.

■

What do you call an Enderman in the Taiga?
Lost!

■

What should you do if you find gravel cliffs in the Nether?
Stay away from them!

What do you call a room with no windows or doors?
A Mushroom!

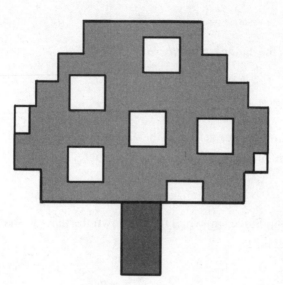

Why did Steve fly to a remote biome?
Because it was too far to walk.

Where would you find an ocean liner in *Minecraft*?
In the desert—because sand lines the ocean.

When Steve was broke he went to the desert. Why?
To look for sand dollars.

What's the capital of *Minecraft*?
The M!

Why didn't Steve starve in the Desert?
Because of all the sand . . . which is there.

What did Steve say when he fell down the narrow shaft?
"I'm all in!"

Which is the funniest biome?
Any of the Hills. They're hill-arious!

It's really cold in the Icy Biome.
Snow joke. It's just really cold there.

Where would you go for fun in the sun, except there isn't
    much sun so it's not much fun?
Cold Beach.

■

Why are *Minecraft* caves so dark?
Because they block out the light!

■

Where will you always find a Minecrafter?
Hanging around on corners.

■

What's the problem with deep *Minecraft* caves?
They drive you batty.

■

Where do Minecrafters get their taxes done?
H&R Block.

■

What could you call a Villager's hut?
A panic room.

This is Steve's favorite kind of dancing.
Square dancing.

Why did Steve go to bed?
Because the bed wouldn't go to him.

What cannot be broken, yet can kill you before you know it?
The Void.

CHAPTER 6

MORE WHAT AM I?

Are you a fun guy? Do you know Fun Gus? This biome may
be just right for you! What am I?
Mushroom Island.

■

Sometimes I'm green, sometimes I'm yellow. But I'm never
red, so I'm not a traffic light. What am I?
An Experience Orb.

■

I plow and plow but never sow. What am I?
A Pig.

■

I make my lair out of string and catch my prey with a bite . . .
or a sting. What am I?
A Spider.

I wear a coat in the winter and pants in the summer. What am I?
A Dog.

Alive without breath, cold as death.
Never thirsty, but always drinking.
What am I?
Silverfish.

I can swim or walk for miles.
I'm big with thick, white hair.
What am I?
A Polar Bear.

I always leaf and am there when things get punchy. What am I?
A Tree.

■

I am a hunk. Or a slice. Or a chunk. Or a piece.
What am I?
A Slab.

■

I am *not* a fan of water. What am I?
Enderman, Snowman, Blaze, Slime, Magma Cube . . .

■

No armor, enchantment or weapon can stop me. The cure is
so simple. What am I?
Hunger.

■

A world of green contains a world of red, spotted with black
and white freckles. What am I?
A Watermelon.

I am highly sought after by every man. And yet I have no
worth or special purpose. What am I?
Dragon egg.

I make color, but I am gray. What am I?
Squid.

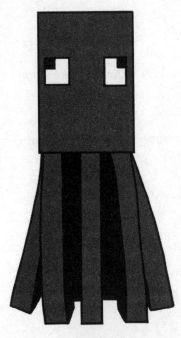

Rain, rain, go away, come back another day, says I. What am I?
A Husk.

Why hadn't Steve slept in days?
Because he sleeps nights.

What runs around a field but doesn't move?
A fence!

What changes on its own every seven days, but only for ten seconds when you try to change it?
The weather.

What falls, but never breaks? What breaks, but never falls?
Day and night.

Steve built a one-story house. There were all kinds of rooms, and a tower, and hundreds of torches. Where did he put the stairs?
Nowhere, because it was a one-story house!

What made Alex suddenly stand still, completely frozen
where she stood?
The pause button!

What are the happiest flowers in *Minecraft*?
Dandy-lions.

The red house is made of red bricks.
The blue house is made of blue bricks.
What is the greenhouse made of?
Glass!

How do you make a goldfish age?
Take out the "g."

I used to be on paper, now I'm totally electronic. And I can
always show you the right way. What am I?
A map.

I see you, but do not speak, only wave. What am I?
The Ocean.

Only after you grab this tool can you take your pick. What
am I?
A Pickaxe.

You can fight or hunt with words, so long as you rearrange
me first. What am I?
Sword. (Move the "s" on "words" to the front of "word," and
you get "sword"!)

I am a transparent tool, but I am not a Glass Bottle. What am I?
Shears.

I'm usually the sign that things are over, but in *Minecraft*
I'm just the beginning. What am I?
The End.

We're part of a neighborhood or a city, but you'll find us in
even the most empty space in *Minecraft*. What are we?
Blocks!

I help you live by *not* living. What am I?
An animal in Minecraft.

I may look like a Tree, but I am not covered in leaves. What
am I?
A Creeper.

Enter me, the time is three. Exit me, the time is . . . three?!
What am I?
The Nether.

I am alive, but I am dead. How can this be? What happened
to me?
It's a Zombie.

I am alive, but I am dead. You never "sausage" a sight!
Zombie Pigman.

■

In trying to vanquish you, I vanquish myself. It's so
frustrating I could explode! What am I?
A Creeper.

■

I am full of Trees, but I am not the Forest. What am I?
The Jungle.

■

If you shout out, "Hey, you," we will come even though you
didn't call us. Who are we?
*A Horse and a Sheep. (We thought you said "hay" and
"ewe.")*

■

With just a small addition, a Minecrafter could eat me. What
am I?
Desert. (Desert + s = dessert.)

Alone we are cold, but when we get together we make sparks fly! What are we?
Flint and Steel.

I come from the Void . . . and "avoid" me is what you ought to do. What am I?
Enderman.

I am a weapon, but you cannot build me or find me, for you already have me. What am I?
Fists.

I provide protection from the Void, but you cannot "rest" on me. What am I?
Bedrock.

I am a fire-man . . . but I don't put out fires. What am I?
Blaze.

I am very useful, but can also be a real "pane." What am I?
A glass block.

I am very hard to find, and if a friend has me you'll be green
with envy—but not as green as me. What am I?
An emerald block.

We're very good at spelling, but you won't find us in any
school or spelling bee. What are we?
Witches.

We're useless alone, and our names even rhyme. We just
belong together. What are we?
Bow and arrow.

We don't have any "body." No bones about it. What are we?
Skeletons.

In the real world, you'd find us on the back of a horse, but in *Minecraft* we ride upon monsters, of course. What are we?
Spider Jockeys.

We'll show you what "fun guys" we can be . . . if you give us plenty of "room." What are we?
Mushrooms.

Feed me lava or milk. I can handle either! What am I?
A Bucket.

Are we the most valuable fish in *Minecraft*? Sure, because there are no goldfish in *Minecraft*! What are we?
Silverfish.

I am the only thing separating your Overwold from the darkness of the Void. What am I?
Bedrock.

I am the only thing that can destroy Bedrock. What am I?
Nothing!

Grass won't grow on me, but other plants can. What am I?
Podzol.

When you destroy me, I fall to pieces. Still, you cannot
    rebuild me. What am I?
Glass.

■

Once I die, my secret becomes known to you. What am I?
Enderdragon.

■

I am known to be harmless, yet, I am not defenseless. What
    am I?
Pigman.

■

Souls are trapped in me, and can never get out. What am I?
Soul Sand.

■

The most ruthless and the most rare. You may think I'm
    harmless, but you're off by just a hare.
What am I?
Killer Bunny.

CHAPTER 7

TOOLING AROUND

Animals drop things. What does Steve drop?
Anvils.

What do cutting tools say when they share a drink?
"Shears!"

What kind of fish do Minecrafters eat?
Smelt.

Alex: Who left all this stone in the furnace?
Steve: Whoever smelt it, dealt it!

Why should you worry about crafters who use anvils?
Because they're anvillains!

◼

What did Steve say to the Torch?
"You light up my life!"

Why did Steve have to go back home for his tools?
Because he got benched.

Why didn't Steve's minecart work?
Because it was tired.

■

Was the Torch happy when it was extinguished?
Yes, it was de-lighted!

■

What happened to Steve's house when he installed a torch?
It became a light-house!

■

Why couldn't Steve stop fishing?
Once he started, he got hooked.

■

What's the fastest tool in *Minecraft*?
The clocks—they're always running.

■

How do you make a stool in *Minecraft*?
Just sit on a Mushroom—it's a toadstool!

What kind of ruler is the difference between life and death?
A health meter.

Why was the Torch uptight?
Because it needed to lighten up.

Where do Minecrafters go for extra cash?
The spawn shop.

Why was Steve mad at a Tree?
He had an Axe to grind.

Why did the Minecrafter run away with a light source?
Because it was a Torch-and-go situation.

Why was the Redstone sad?
It was tired of getting picked on.

Where do tools stay when they're on vacation?
At a hoe-tel.

■

Do hippies like *Minecraft*?
Yeah, mine, they totally dig it.

■

What happened when Steve got way too deep underground?
He could feel his cart pounding.

■

What did one Torch say to the other Torch?
"Do you wanna go out tonight?"

■

Why didn't Steve bother with the train tracks?
He just didn't have the cart.

■

How do you ask a question in *Minecraft*?
You send a quarry.

What do you call a torch on the ceiling?
A high light.

■

This tool is all-encompassing but it only does one thing.
    What is it?
A compass.

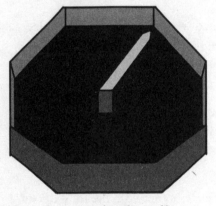

What did one Sword say to other Sword?
"You're looking sharp!"

■

How do Minecrafters send letters?
With an axe machine.

If it took eight men ten hours to build a wall, how long
    would it take four men to build it?
No time at all, since the wall is already built!

■

What bow has no arrows?
A rainbow!

■

How do you learn more about *Minecraft* tools?
Axe questions!

■

What do you call a Lever that doesn't work?
A severed Lever.

■

Why did Steve swallow his own Clock at sundown?
He needed a night watchman.

■

Where do young Minecrafters go before they become miners?
To tool!

Why did Steve chop down a Tree?
It was knotty.

■

What would you call the history of a minecart?
An auto-biography.

■

After punching trees, why did Steve grab a clock?
Because time heals all wounds.

■

Where does a Minecrafter go to get their shoes repaired?
A cobbler.

■

What did Alex say when she offered Steve a bunch of Axes?
"Take your pick!"

■

What did Steve do when he felt ill?
He built a dock-tor.

Steve punched down a tree and then asked it how it felt. How did the tree respond?

It didn't—it was stumped.

What do you call a boat in *Minecraft*?

A *Minecraft* Raft.

Why do Shears make good cart drivers?
They know all the shortcuts!

■

How did Steve and Alex decide who got to mine first?
They played Stone, Paper, Shears!

■

Why did Steve go to the dentist?
For an extraction.

■

How do Minecrafters party?
They raise the roof!

■

Why did nosey Steve build such a bad roof?
He kept eavesdropping.

■

What did Alex do when Steve gave her a diamond ring?
She mined obsidian with it.

Why did Steve give his Cow a hammer at night time?
It was time for it to hit the hay!

Where did Steve find a helping hand?
At the end of his arm.

What did Steve say as he dug into a giant shaft?
"Let's get to the bottom of this!"

What did Steve do when his life meter was low and he
thought he was dying?
He built a living room.

Why did Steve build a place for horses?
He wanted something stable in his life.

Why did Steve build a suit of Armor?
Because he needed a knight gown.

Why did Santa start playing *Minecraft*?
To get a hoe-hoe-hoe.

What do you call a miner without an eye?
A mner.

Why couldn't Steve lift his treasure?
He had Chest pains.

What's the problem with finding diamonds near lava?
You get rich or die trying.

Why did Steve win a debate with a Diamond Sword?
He had a good point.

Why are Minecrafters so selfish?
Because everything is always "mine, mine, mine!"

How do Minecrafters pick their noses?
With a Pickaxe!

What kind of jokes do Minecrafters like best?
Swordplay.

What can you put in stone to make it lighter?
A hole.

What do you get when you cross TNT and Ice?
Chaos!

What kind of car would the female protagonist of *Minecraft*
drive?
Alex's.

What kind of dinosaurs would you find in *Minecraft*?
Dino-mite.

■

What's the very first thing you see in *Minecraft*?
M!

CHAPTER 8

PASSIVE MOBS AND CUDDLY CREATURES

Why can't you complain when you haven't spawned any Cows?
Because you've got no beef!

Where do all the Cows in *Minecraft* go when they're not on
screen?
The mooooovies.

Why are Squid so imposing?
Because they're well-armed!

How can you tell if a Squid likes you?
He'll ink at you!

How do Snow Golems get around?
Via icicle.

How do you make a Squid laugh?
With ten-tickles!

What would you call a dumb Squid?
A squidiot.

What did the Squid say when he dropped an item?
"Just squidding!"

What happened when the Squid found some gold?
Inky ingots!

What do you call an Snow Golem with a tool?
An ice-sickle

How does a Golem get bigger?
By pumping Iron!

How do Sheep love to waste time?
By watching Ewe-Tube.

What do you call a resident of a chilly biome?
You call em' Golems!

How does a Snow Golem find its home biome?
He finds it to be brrrr-fect!

A bunch of Cows wandered away from Farmland.
It was an udder catastrophe.

What happens when you cross a Snow Golem with an Iron Golem?
You get a puddle.

What's another way to make a Water Block?
Take a Snow Golem to the Desert.

What did the Snow Golem's mom call him?
Her little pumpkinhead!

Where do all the Mules go when you don't need them?
To the Mule-seum.

Can a Polar Bear build a *Minecraft* house?
Sure, igloos it together.

How do you call a Polar Bear wearing earmuffs?
You don't—he can't hear you!

What do you call a Cow that doesn't do anything?
A Milk Dud!

How do you communicate with Fish?
Drop them a line.

What is leather used for most in *Minecraft*?
Holding the Cows together!

Are Cows the best animal in *Minecraft*?
Whatever, it's a moooot point.

What happened when the Ocelot wandered onto the beach
   biome?
Sandy Claws!

■

What do you get when you cross an Evoker with an Snow
   Golem?
Frostbite.

■

When a Rabbit drops a Rabbit's foot, it's lucky for all but
   who?
The Rabbit!

■

What kind of shows do NPCs like?
Talk shows.

■

How do you make fir trees in *Minecraft*?
Put a rabbit in a tree.

Did you hear about the Rabbit that didn't notice the garden
  of free food?
It's like he didn't carrot all!

How do you make a hedgehog in *Minecraft*?
Throw a Pig into some hedges.

Where can you find a horse in *Minecraft*?
In their neigh-borhood.

Why won't Bats take sides in an argument?
They prefer to stay neutral.

How do you summon your horse?
"Hay!"

What did the Snow Golem say to the Torch?
"I melt when I'm around you!"

Where in *Minecraft* would you shear a sheep?
At the baa-baa shop.

What happens if you cross a Chicken with some Ore?
You get a featherweight boxer.

Do all the sheep in *Minecraft* look the same?
Yep—they're ewe-niform.

Why do white sheep eat more grass than dyed sheep?
Because there are more of them!

What do you get when you cross a Chicken with a Clock?
A cluck.

What do you get when you cross a Chicken with TNT?
Cock-a-doodle-boom!

What kind of dogs do Minecrafters like best?
Boxers.

What letter do you get when you've got two sheep?
W (Double-ewe).

Why is it nice to encounter rabbits?
Because they're so hoppy!

Cow #1: Did you know all cows in *Minecraft* are female?
Cow #2: Really?
Cow #1: Yep, no bull!

Why was the Chicken happy?
Everything was egg-cellent.

Why are Cows unreliable?
They're just so grazy!

How do you catch a unique Rabbit?
Unique up on him.

What did the sheep say after trying to eat a cactus?
Accidents Wool happen!

What does a Chicken drop after it eats Iron?
Chicken nuggets.

What do you call a boat full of Sheep with Swords?
A battlesheep!

What do Snow Golems clean with?
A brr-oom!

Why did Steve build a Chicken coop with only two doors?
Because if it had four doors, it would've been a sedan!

What do you get when a Chicken eats a bunch of ore?
A brick-layer!

■

Alex's shelter was chicken-proof.
Yep, it was im-peckable.

■

What do you call a sleeping Cow?
A bull-dozer.

What can't add, but can definitely multiply?
Rabbits.

Why did the Ocelot go to the cleaners?
To remove its spots.

Where do Ocelots shop?
Cat-alogs.

Why are the Cows in *Minecraft* so happy?
Because every day is a moo day.

What's the loudest animal in *Minecraft*?
The blah blah black Sheep.

What kind of teeth live in the coldest biomes?
Molar bears.

A horse is tied to a fifteen-foot rope and there is a bale of hay
twenty feet away. The horse, however, is still able to eat
from the hay. How is this possible?
The rope wasn't tied to anything!

■

Dogs have fleas. What do Sheep have?
Fleece.

■

What did the Dog say when he sat on a rough plank?
Rough!

■

Can Ocelots sing?
Sure, they're very mewsical.

■

When's the best time of day to spawn Cows?
In the moooonlight.

■

Why are Bats hard to be around?
Because they have Bat breath.

Why was the Rabbit unhappy?
It was having a bad hare day.

Why can't Ocelots play Hide-and-Seek?
They're always spotted.

What do you call a Chicken in the Tundra?
A brrrrrd!

How do you make a porcupine in *Minecraft*?
Cross a pig with a tree. Get it?

What animal can jump higher than the highest building you
can build in *Minecraft*?
Any or all of them—buildings can't jump!

What kind of Chicken drops blue feathers?
A sad one.

What happened to the Sheep that stepped on a flower?
It dyed.

Did you hear about the mean *Minecraft* sheep?
It was a real Wooly Bully.

Why are Chickens so cool?
Because they wear feather jackets.

Why do Squid like salt water?
Because pepper makes them sneeze.

What's Herobrine's favorite kind of music?
Rock and troll!

CHAPTER 9
SWIFTLY, ALEX!

"I just love putting up the supports for my structure!" Alex beamed.

"There are Chickens in my yard!" clucked Alex cockily.

"This Cow never runs out of milk," Alex uttered continuously.

"Creepers are always showing up," said Alex incidentally.

"I've got to fix the cart," said Alex mechanically.

"I wish it was still night time," Alex mourned.

"I need to sleep," said Alex, nodding.

"I have more windows than I need," said Alex painfully.

"I wouldn't work Glass blocks with my hands," said Alex painstakingly.

"I've just cut myself with a Pickaxe!" said Alex pointedly.

"The door is over there," Alex pointed out.

■

"My sword is dull," said Alex pointlessly.

"All my flowers died," said Alex witheringly.

■

"Stop that horse!" cried Alex with woe.

"Let's go tame one," said Alex wolfishly.

■

"This river is rough," said Alex rapidly.

■

"There's that Enderman again!" Alex recited.

■

"I'm measuring for my shelter again," Alex remarked.

■

"I'm not going to build beyond this point," Alex ruled.

■

"Can I use this Sword yet?" Alex cut in sharply.

■

"I'm very strong!" said Alex soberly.

■

"Get to the back of the boat," said Alex sternly.

■

"This shaft is infested," said Alex trenchantly.

"This isn't a real Emerald," said Alex stonily.

"I've brought back the Cart I borrowed," said Alex truculently.

■

"I don't think I'll eat any Fish today," said Alex unerringly.

■

"I flew from one biome to the other," said Alex, visibly moved.

■

"Every second in *Minecraft* feels like it lasts for seven days," said Alex in a moment of weakness.

CHAPTER 10

YOU KNOW YOU'RE A MINECRAFTER IF . . .

The craft store is not what you were expecting.

■

You've asked your parents how babies spawn.

■

When you played with blocks as a toddler, you built a fully immersive world filled with creatures.

■

You're jealous of the cat for getting to play in a literal sandbox.

■

Your favorite rapper is Ice Cube.

You'd rather have Desert than dessert.

■

You watch *The Flintstones* just for the bedrock.

■

You don't build snowmen, you build golems.

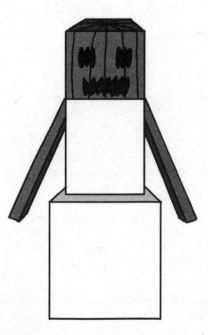

You call your pen an ink sac.

You're surprised when your real-life wooden pickaxe is useless.

You think *Bob the Builder* could work a little faster.

You're disappointed that "heart of gold" is only an expression.

You've tried to build a wall out of walnuts.

You think Notch should be on Mount Rushmore.

You've offered to cut down the family Christmas tree. With your hands.

You've suggested that your school go to a "block schedule."

A game of Jenga with you takes hours.

You'll play a dice game, but only so you can stack the dice.

When you go to a national monument, you're on the lookout for Guardians.

You assume anybody named Johnny is a Vindicator.

You can't listen to music with horns because you think it means a Vex is nearby.

■

You want to study geology in college.

■

You turn down the chance to go on a treasure hunt to stay home and play *Minecraft*.

■

You don't find the Great Wall of China to be particularly impressive.

■

You keep getting in trouble for putting things in the furnace.

■

When someone asks for a glass of water, you give them some sand and point them to the oven.

All you want to do at the beach is make sand castles.

You prefer all surfaces to be stained.

■

Whenever you hear counting, you duck because you think TNT is about to explode.

■

You call all boys "Steve" and all girls "Alex."

CHAPTER 11

KNOCK-KNOCK . . .

Knock-knock . . .
Who's there?
Wood.
Wood who?
Wood you please open the door?

Knock-knock . . .
Who's there?
Wither.
Wither who?
I'm coming in, Wither you like it or not!

Knock-knock . . .
Who's there?
Everest.
Everest who?
Everest, or is it just build, build, build?

Knock-knock . . .
Who's there?
Endermite.
Endermite who?
Open the door, Endermite not kill you!

Knock-knock . . .
Who's there?
Juicy.
Juicy who?
Juicy any Creepers around?

Knock-knock . . .
Who's there?
Donut.
Donut who?
Donut open the door—there are Hostiles around!

■

Knock-knock . . .
Who's there?
Peas.
Peas who?
Peas come outside and help me dig!

■

Knock-knock . . .
Who's there?
Alex.
Alex who?
Alex plain when you open the door!

■

Knock-knock . . .
Who's there?
Alex.
Alex who?
Hey, Alex the questions!

Knock-knock . . .
Who's there?
Macon.
Macon who?
Stand back, I'm Macon my own way in!

Knock-knock . . .
Who's there?
Megan.
Megan who?
Megan stuff in *Minecraft* is the best!

Knock-knock . . .
Who's there?
Zany.
Zany who?
Zany body wanna go for a dig?

■

Knock-knock . . .
Who's there?
Norway.
Norway who?
Norway I'm staying out here with all these Zombies and
   Skeletons!

■

Knock-knock . . .
Who's there?
Allison.
Allison who?
Allison for hissing, and if I hear it, can I come in?

■

Knock-knock . . .
Who's there?
Gwen.
Gwen who?
Gwen do you think you want to play *Minecraft*?

■

Knock-knock . . .
Who's there?
Interrupting Blaze.
Interruping Bla—
Sizzle . . .

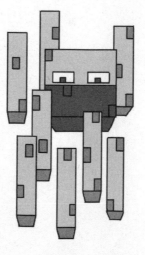

Knock-knock . . .
Who's there?
Interrupting Ghast.
Interrupting Gha—
Chirp-chirp!

Knock-knock . . .
Who's there?
Boat.
Boat who?
Boat time you got out here and mined!

Knock-knock . . .
Who's there?
Seed.
Seed who?
Seeds spawn!

Knock-knock . . .
Who's there?
Iguana.
Iguana who?
Iguana come in and play *Minecraft*!

■

Knock-knock . . .
Who's there?
Raven.
Raven who?
I've been raven about *Minecraft* to all my friends!

■

Knock-knock . . .
Who's there?
Al.
Al who?
Al give you some Ore if you let me in!

■

Knock-knock . . .
Who's there?
Denise.
Denise who?
Denise hurt from where the Skeleton shot me!

Knock-knock . . .
Who's there?
Canoe.
Canoe who?
Canoe give me some gems?

Knock-knock . . .
Who's there?
Iva.
Iva who?
Iva sore hand from punching trees!

Knock-knock . . .
Who's there?
Dishes.
Dishes who?
Dissssshes a Creeper. *BOOM!*

Knock-knock . . .
Who's there?
Husk.
Husk who?
Bless you!

Knock-knock . . .
Who's there?
Biome.
Biome who?
Why would I Biome when I can build one?

Knock-knock . . .
Who's there?
Guardian.
Guardian who?
Guardian your shelter, there are laser-shooting fish out here!

Knock-knock . . .
Who's there?
Fish.
Fish who?
Fish who shoot lasers!

Knock-knock . . .
Who's there?
Geno.
Geno who?
Geno any good *Minecraft* tips?

Knock-knock . . .
Who's there?
Barry.
Barry who?
Barry the treasure before anyone can steal it!

■

Knock-knock . . .
Who's there?
Cow.
Cow who?
Cowhide!

■

Knock-knock . . .
Who's there?
Sadie.
Sadie who?
Sadie air is hot in this Desert!

■

Knock-knock . . .
Who's there?
Kenya.
Kenya who?
I've fallen in a shaft, Kenya help me?

■

Knock-knock . . .
Who's there?
Broken Sword.
Broken Sword who?
Ah, it's pointless.

■

Knock-knock . . .
Who's there?
Ivan.
Ivan who?
Ivan working hard on my shelter!

■

Knock-knock . . .
Who's there?
Ivana.
Ivana who?
Ivana get you, because this is a Wither!

■

Knock-knock . . .
Who's there?
Wanda.
Wanda who?
Wanda where I left my tools.

■

Knock-knock . . .
Who's there?
Wooden Axe.
Wooden Axe who?
Wooden Axe me twice next time, wood you?

■

Knock-knock . . .
Who's there?
Witch.
Witch who?
Witch you would let me in!

Knock-knock . . .
Who's there?
Hurd.
Hurd who?
I Hurd my hand punching trees and it hurts to knock!

Knock-knock . . .
Who's there?
Coal Mine.
Coal Mine who?
Coal mines are just waiting for us to dig in!

Knock-knock . . .
Who's there?
May.
May who?
May I borrow a Torch, please?

■

Knock-knock . . .
Who's there?
Coal.
Coal who?
It's so Coal out here!

■

Knock-knock . . .
Who's there?
Ewe.
Ewe who?
Ewe've made your bed, now Sheep in it.

■

Knock-knock . . .
Who's there?
Havana.
Havana who?
Havana wonderful time playing *Minecraft*?

Knock-knock . . .
Who's there?
Olive.
Olive who?
Olive playing *Minecraft*!

Knock-knock . . .
Who's there?
Huron.
Huron who?
Huron the spot I wanted to build!

Knock-knock . . .
Who's there?
Thumping.
Thumping who?
Thumping just stole your Emeralds!

Knock-knock . . .
Who's there?
Scold.
Scold who?
Scold out here in the Ice Biome!

Knock-knock . . .
Who's there?
Philip.
Philip my chest with emeralds, please!

Knock-knock . . .
Who's there?
Tamara.
Tamara who?
Tamara we'll build something new together!

■

Knock-knock . . .
Who's there?
Aardvark.
Aardvark who?
Aardvark a million miles to play *Minecraft*!

■

Knock-knock . . .
Who's there?
Canoe.
Canoe who?
Canoe lend me some tools?

■

Knock-knock . . .
Who's there?
Formosa.
Formosa who?
Formosa the summer I played *Minecraft*.

■

Knock-knock . . .
Who's there?
Disguise.
Disguise who?
Disguise a big fan of *Minecraft*!

■

Knock-knock . . .
Who's there?
Jamaica.
Jamaica who?
Jamaica huge tower yet?

■

Knock-knock . . .
Who's there?
Jim.
Jim who?
Jim mind if I come in and play *Minecraft?*

■

Knock-knock . . .
Who's there?
Handsome.
Handsome who?
Handsome of those Emeralds to me!

■

Knock-knock . . .
Who's there?
Doug.
Doug who?
I Doug deep and still couldn't find any Emeralds!

■

Knock-knock . . .
Who's there?
House.
House who?
House is great, you build it yourself?

Knock-knock . . .
Who's there?
Wayne.
Wayne who?
The Wayne is coming down, let me in!

Knock-knock . . .
Who's there?
Guitar.
Guitar who?
Let's guitar Pickaxes and go find some Diamonds!

Knock-knock . . .
Who's there?
Stew.
Stew who?
Stew you want me to make you a Mushroom Stew?

Knock-knock . . .
Who's there?
Water.
Water who?
Water Blocks!

Knock-knock . . .
Who's there?
Ida.
Ida who?
Ida called first, but there are no phones in *Minecraft*!

Knock-knock . . .
Who's there?
Stan.
Stan who?
Stan back, I'm going to break that Pressure Plate!

■

Knock-knock . . .
Who's there?
Interrupting Zombie.
Interrupting Zombie who?
Braaaains!

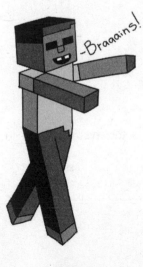

-Braaaains!

Knock-knock . . .
Who's there?
Weird.
Weird who?
Weird you hide the Diamonds?

Knock-knock . . .
Who's there?
Dishes.
Dishes who?
Dishes Alex, open up!

Knock-knock . . .
Who's there?
Rock
Rock who?
"Rock a bye baby in the treetop . . ."

Knock-knock . . .
Who's there?
Zombies.
Zombies who?
Zombies make honey, others don't.

■

Knock-knock . . .
Who's there?
Alpaca.
Alpaca who?
Alpaca chest full of Emeralds for you!

■

Knock-knock . . .
Who's there?
Clara.
Clara who?
Clara space and let's build something new!

■

Knock-knock . . .
Who's there?
Anita.
Anita who?
Anita borrow a Pickaxe!

Knock-knock . . .
Who's there?
Pig.
Pig who?
Pig up all your Emeralds or you're going to lose them!

Knock-knock . . .
Who's there?
Xavier.
Xavier who?
Xavier self—there are hostiles everywhere!

Knock-knock . . .
Who's there?
Needle.
Needle who?
Needle light? Get a Torch!

Knock-knock . . .
Who's there?
Crash!
Oh no, I played on hard mode!

Knock-knock . . .
Who's there?
Ocelot.
Ocelot who?
You Ocelot of questions!

CHAPTER 12
JUST PLAIN DUMB

Where does Steve buy his blue pants?
At the blue pants store.

How does a miner go to the bathroom in an Enderportal?
In a portal-potty.

This is the coldest version of *Minecraft*.
Minedraft.

Where does soul sand grow?
Nether. You mind?

Why do cows have bells?
Their horns don't work.

Why was Steve so good at yoga?
Because he lived in the right Bi-ohm.

How you make a pincushion in *Minecraft*?
Run through a group of skeletons.

How can pigs fly?
Apply enough TNT.

Why is *Minecraft* made of blocks?
You can't build with circles.

How many tickles does it take to make a Squid laugh?
Ten-ticles.

What's the best way to catch a fish in *Minecraft*?
Have another player throw one at you.

How do you count your Cows?
With a cow-culator.

What kind of snake plays *Minecraft*?
A boa constructor.

Who built the first tunnel in *Minecraft*?
A worm, probably!

What did the farming Villager grow after he worked very hard?
Tired.

What in *Minecraft* is brown and sticky?
A stick.

■

What's the dirtiest thing in *Minecraft*?
Dirt.

■

What's the hardest thing in *Minecraft*?
The rocks.

■

What's the hardest mode in *Minecraft*?
Hard mode.

■

Why is *Minecraft* child's play?
Because all you have to do is play with blocks!

■

How do you bring about peace?
Play *Minecraft* on Peaceful Mode.

Why was Steve holding a carrot in his hand?
He must have eaten his Pickaxe for lunch.

◼

How can you tell if a Cow is male or female?
If you're playing *Minecraft*, it's female.

◼

What's the one thing about digging a hole in *Minecraft*?
It's so boring.

◼

How do you stop a boat in *Minecraft*?
Sing "whoa whoa whoa, the boat . . . "

◼

What do you get when you pound Ores together?
Rock music.

◼

Why is Notch so cool?
Because he has millions of fans.

Steve wasn't always a confident miner, you know.
First he had to get a little boulder.

■

Which side of a Rabbit is the furriest?
The outside.

■

What did one Ore say to the other Ore?
Nothing. Ore doesn't talk.

■

How did they decide to add polar bears to *Minecraft*?
They took a North Poll.

■

What did one hay bale say to the other hay bale?
"Hay, bale!"

■

What did the Grass say to the Dirt?
"I've got you covered!"

What kind of trees grow on a miner's hands?
Palm trees!

What's a Tree's favorite drink?
Root beer.

What's a Tree's least favorite drink?
Punch!

Why is Grass so dangerous?
Because it's full of blades!

What is a Tree's least favorite month?
Sep-timber.

Where do you find an ocean without water?
On a map!

Is the world round or flat?
In *Minecraft*? Neither!

■

What did Steve say when he walked into a tower?
"Ouch!"

■

What in *Minecraft* gets bigger the more you take away from it?
A hole!

■

If a Tree had a watch and checked it, what would it say?
Tree o'clock!

■

What did the floor say to the ceiling?
"Stop looking at me!"

■

What did one Ice block say to another Ice block?
"You are so cool!"

Why did the Ice block strike up the conversation?
Because it was an ice thing to do.

What did Steve say when he fell into a mineshaft?
"Well, I guess I've hit rock bottom."

Why did Steve build a shelter on flat land?
Because it was flat.

What's the wettest thing in *Minecraft*?
A Water Block.

What's shinier than a diamond in *Minecraft*?
Two diamonds.

What do you call a Cow with seven legs?
A seven-legged Cow.

What did Steve say when he lost his Pickaxe?
"Where's my Pickaxe?"

Why did Steve put a Clock under his Workbench?
So he could have more time to build stuff.

Pretend you're surrounded by 100 skeletons and 200 creepers.
    What do you do?
Stop pretending!

When is a Minecart not a Minecart?
When it turns into a shaft.

Does a Skeleton Horse have any meat?
Neigh.

What in *Minecraft* is not so super-secret?
The super-secret settings.

What did Steve say to the Jack o' Lantern?
"Face it!"

What would you find on Farmland?
Farmers.

The only bars in *Minecraft*: iron bars.

What did Steve say when he saw a bunch of buildings?
"This is quite the development."

What shoe size does Steve wear?
Two square feet.

What should you do if you don't like the weather in *Minecraft*?
Change your altitude!

What's blue and turquoise and blue and turquoise and blue
and turquoise and . . . ?
Steve falling down a hill.

How did Steve jump off a ladder without hurting himself?
He jumped off the bottom rung.

What happened when Steve listened to a Torch?
He burned his ear.

What will you find in every Village?
The town square.

What else will you find in the Village?
Villagers!

165

A man walked into an Iron Bar.
It hurt.

■

Why should you never let an Iron Golem hold your father?
Because they drop poppies!

■

Which *Minecraft* flower has a mouth?
The two-lips.

■

What's brown, messy, and everywhere in *Minecraft*?
Dirt.

■

What's one amazing thing you can do in the real world that
you can't do in *Minecraft*?
Play *Minecraft!*

■

We'd tell you another shelter construction joke . . .
. . . but we're still working on it!

What big scary animal could you build in *Minecraft*?
A rockodile.

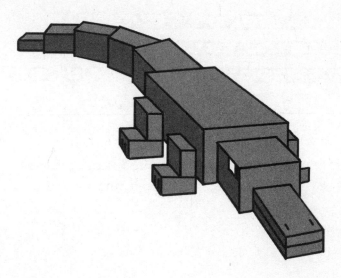

CHAPTER 13

MINECRAFT CRACKS AND WITTY WORDS OF WISDOM

Why is *Minecraft* always getting better? Because you can't "block" progress. Or then again, maybe you can . . .

■

The best part of *Minecraft*? The hole thing!

■

We'd tell you a story about how to beat *Minecraft,* but it might drag-on.

■

Is there more than one kind of dirt in *Minecraft*? Of coarse there is!

Sticks and stones may break your bones . . . and so will Zombies and Skeletons.

Ocelots are like potato chips. You can never have just one!

Geniuses enjoy playing *Minecraft*. They like mine games!

■

If life gives you lemons, well, you probably modded the game to include those lemons.

■

The place to go in *Minecraft* to get smarter is, of course, the master-mine.

■

Every slime story begins with "Once Upon A Slime."

Succeeding at this game is a simple act of mine over matter.

Minecrafters are often also photographers. They just like to see what develops.

Minecrafters wear boxers. Never briefs.

You play *Minecraft*. Your little brother or sister wants to play *Minecraft* so bad they might as well be playing *Whinecraft*!

Minecrafters don't get the blues—they get Lapiz Lazuli.

When you're in the sandy biomes, everything is Beachy keen!

Those who live in glass houses . . . would probably enjoy *Minecraft*.

Your *Minecraft* structures should win an award . . . for being outstanding in its field.

■

Hostiles might just be big fans of Steve and Alex. They're always "mobbing" them!

■

It's not hard to spot an Ocelot. They already come that way.

■

Playing *Minecraft* beats being a toddler. You don't have to choose between playing with blocks or playing with the sandbox. *Minecraft* is both!

■

When the moon comes up in the game, it's like a difference between night and day!

■

Minecraft: Before you can load your lode, you've got to let the code load!

Minecraft: You don't become a master right away. You build to it.

■

You can't get water from a stone . . . but you can put them next to each other in *Minecraft* and see what happens.

■

The path to a mine in *Minecraft* is merely the road to the lode!

■

Don't trust an Enderman. You can see right through them!

■

What's the great thing about the different types of *Minecraft* games? Whatever the mode, there's always a lode!

■

How is *Minecraft* better than ancient Rome? Because Rome wasn't built in a day, but you can build anything on *Minecraft* in minutes.

Minecrafters make great waiters and waitresses because they're familiar with servers.

∎

The best and worst thing about *Minecraft*? The pitfalls.

∎

Minecraft pigs are major blockheads.

∎

If Christopher Columbus had been a Minecrafter, he might have set out to prove the world was square!

∎

What do Notch and the Pilgrims have in common? Both made quite a life for themselves out of rocks—Notch with digitized ones, and the Pilgrims after they landed at Plymouth Rock.

∎

Did you hear what happened to the Minecrafter who played for too long? She went wall-eyed!

174

"Three's company!" Sounds like something a Wither says!

■

Minecraft is the only place where getting stuck between a rock and a hard place is a good thing!

■

We'd tell you a joke about the *Minecraft* mountains . . . but you wouldn't get over it.

■

Calling someone a "square" is an insult to everyone but a Minecrafter. And Steve. And Alex.

■

"You're crushing it" is a compliment in real life. Not so much in *Minecraft!*

■

Minecraft is the best source of exercise there is! Why, there's walking, running, flying, swinging tools . . .

Friendships like Diamond Pickaxes: Take it slow and they'll last a lifetime.

Some Minecrafters don't go to another dimension because they Nether have the time.

You won't be good at *Minecraft* right away. You'll get there, bit by bit.

To get good at *Minecraft,* you just have to be in the right mine-set.

The tallest building you could ever build in *Minecraft*? Why, that would be the library, because it has so many stories!

With *Minecraft,* you can be there *and* be square!

Steve followed Alex to a new area, because they were friends till The End.

■

Alex and Steve survived The End . . . because everything always turns out alright in The End.

■

And finally, do you want to hear the world's longest *Minecraft* joke?
Here it comes.
Are you ready?
Okay.
Here it is.
Here is the world's longest *Minecraft* joke:
"The world's longest *Minecraft* joke."